Original title:

Pollen in the Air

Copyright © 2025 Creative Arts Management OÜ
All rights reserved.

Author: Penelope Hawthorne
ISBN HARDBACK: 978-1-80566-752-0
ISBN PAPERBACK: 978-1-80566-822-0

Echoes of the Flowering Cloud

Tiny dancers swirl about,
Tickling noses, causing doubt.
Sneezes sound like giggles loud,
Nature's joke—what a crowd!

Floating whispers, golden cheer,
Hope your allergies aren't near!
A dust of sunshine on the breeze,
Laughing bees and sneezing sneeze.

Fluff balls sailing, tickle fight,
In the sun, they're quite a sight.
The flowers chuckle, all bemused,
While humans hunt for tissues, bruised.

So join the fun, don't despair,
Dance with friends, and shake your hair.
For in this merry, sneezy spree,
Life's a laugh—just wait and see!

Flight of the Floral Whispers

Buzzing bees in floral hats,
Dancing clovers, silly chats.
A dandelion's sneeze is a laugh,
As they scatter like a secret staff.

Butterflies with jokes to share,
Tickling petals, how they dare!
Whispers float on the bright breeze,
Funny tales told by buzzing bees.

A Serenade to Sunkissed Moments

Golden rays and giggles bright,
Sunflowers smile with sheer delight.
A ladybug dons a tiny crown,
Strutting around, never down.

Bees in line do cha-cha dance,
Stumbling once, then take a chance.
Petals blush, oh, what a scene!
Nature's jesters, so serene.

Canvas of Dreams in Bloom

Canvas stretched with hues so wild,
Lazy bumblebees are mild.
Cactus tries to steal the show,
But blooms giggle, 'Oh no, no!'

Tulips wear polka dots with glee,
Whirling amidst the grassy spree.
A rabbit watches, shakes its head,
As every flower dreams in bed.

Flowers' Dance Against the Sun

In the garden, a dance begins,
Daisies giggle, competition spins.
Marigolds twirl, so full of grace,
While crooked stems join in the race.

The sun shines bright on this parade,
With shadows laughing, jokes are laid.
Petals spin and twirl with flair,
A waltz of joy in sunny air.

Whispers of the Yellow Dust

A sneeze echoes through the street,
Nearby, a flower's slight defeat.
Allergies dance with glee tonight,
As noses itch and faces fight.

Tiny warriors hit the ground,
In the air, their giggles sound.
Swirling lightly, with a quirk,
They prank us while we're at work.

Yellow clouds leap from the blooms,
Tickling noses, filling rooms.
Laughter fills the buzzing air,
While sneezing fits are quite the flair.

Who knew nature had such tricks,
With tiny bits that jump and mix?
We stumble, drip, and run around,
In the haze, our joy is found.

Veils of Springtime's Breath

Springtime whispers, soft and bright,
Where noses twitch in sheer delight.
With each breeze, a sprinkle flies,
Mischief lingers as it sighs.

Flowers giggle, giving chase,
Invisible things join the race.
We swat at dreams that float nearby,
While wondering why we blink and cry.

A charming dance of sentient dust,
In this season, it's a must.
Unruly guests on every tree,
They feast on laughter, wild and free.

They mock our sneezes, one by one,
Chasing joy till day is done.
In the air, a jolly jest,
Nature plays, we jest the best.

Dance of the Winged Seeds

Little dancers twirl and spin,
In the sunlight, bright and thin.
They pirouette through casual air,
With giggles loud, they do declare.

Mischief managed on petals soft,
As seeds soar high, or drift aloft.
A frolicsome ballet in the breeze,
Tickling noses, oh what tease!

Each unexpected flick and fall,
Turns our sneezes into a brawl.
With fluttered wisps, they tug and play,
Making us cough and laugh all day.

Amidst the flowers' bright array,
These sprightly seeds like to sway.
In their dance, we laugh and sneeze,
Nature giggles with such ease.

Nature's Sweetest Mist

A fairytale of sneezes grows,
With nature's brew, the mischief flows.
In every corner, laughter swells,
Where flowers hide their tiny spells.

Dusty flurries in the light,
Catch us off guard, oh what a sight!
Pranks around in soft disguise,
While we snort in sweet surprise.

The air's alive with giggling sounds,
Comedic chaos knows no bounds.
Bumblebees chuckle as they zoom,
While we dodge allergens' sweet doom.

A swirl of joy, a sprinkle here,
Can turn our frowns into sheer cheer.
With each breeze, there's joy and jest,
Nature's laughter is the best!

Beyond the Garden's Whisper

Bumblebees buzz like they own the place,
Dancing round flowers with fluttering grace.
They laugh at the humans in their grand hats,
While sipping on nectar like fancy aristocrats.

The roses are blushing, the daisies in cheer,
As dandelions puff like they've drunk too much beer.
The garden's alive with a zany affair,
Nature's own circus, with laughter to spare.

Sunrise's Palette of Fragments

Golden rays spread like spilled paint,
Chasing sleepy bugs whom they treat like a saint.
A ladybug stumbles, a caterpillar grins,
While ants play tag, so no one quite wins.

Colors explode, oh, what a sight!
The early worms wriggle, clinging to light.
They wriggle and giggle, it's all quite absurd,
This early morning show is simply unheard!

The Bounty of Flora's Heart

Petals and leaves engage in a race,
While tiny grasshoppers hop with such grace.
A foxglove is tickled by a passing breeze,
It giggles so hard, it drops to its knees.

Marigolds pop like confetti on air,
Spreading their cheer without a care.
The daisies are chatting, their banter quite grand,
Discussing the latest trends in their land.

Requiem for the Fickle Winds

Oh fickle winds, you flit and you sway,
Stealing my hat, then laughing away.
The butterflies chase you, but trip on a stem,
As daisies just shake their bright little heads.

A dandelion sighs, 'You play far too rough,'
While crickets all chuckle, 'We've quite had enough!'
Yet off goes the breeze, with a wink and a spin,
Leaving behind giggles, oh where do we begin?

Alchemy of Flora and Sky

Dancing daisies in the breeze,
Tickling noses, such a tease.
Bees in bow ties, buzzing quick,
Mixing sunshine, what a trick!

Waving poppies, don't be shy,
They'll send giggles to the sky.
With every sneeze, a laugh erupts,
As nature's joke is well constructed.

The Art of Floral Migrations

Petals hitching a bumbling ride,
On the tails of butterflies wide.
They flit and flutter, such a sight,
A floral flight, oh, what delight!

Dandelions are the best at aims,
Playing scatter, in silly games.
With a puff, they send their cheer,
Wishing all your sneezes here.

Sweet Currents of Existence

Bees on skateboards zoom and glide,
Transporting sweetness, oh what pride!
In this world of tasty treats,
Every bloom has its own beats.

Whisking yellow through the green,
Making nature's dance routine.
Life's a party, let it flow,
In this jam, we steal the show.

Nature's Glittering Confetti

Tiny specks in the sunlight bloom,
A vibrant party, oh such room!
With each gust, a giggle spreads,
Nature's laughter fills our heads.

Kids with hats, they run about,
Catching treasures with a shout.
As the wind plays hide and seek,
Each flower giggles, cheek to cheek.

Floating Dreams of Nature

Tiny specks drift up high,
Balloons without a tie.
They dance and twirl with glee,
Free like a bumblebee.

A sneeze escapes my friend,
As these flakes never end.
He grabs a tissue, oh dear,
Now he can't see the clear!

They swirl like fairy dust,
In this soft gust we trust.
Children chase with sheer delight,
While adults just lose the fight.

As I sip my iced tea,
One lands right on my knee.
"Is this nature's cruel game?"
I laugh, and call its name.

The Breath of Land and Sky

Each field breathes out a sigh,
Sprinkles of gold fly by.
They tickle my nose just so,
Now everyone's in a row!

The wind plays hide and seek,
While I try not to squeak.
A cloud of mischief whirls,
As I dodge tiny pearls.

Why do they make me wheeze?
They float like ladies' keys.
Dramatic coughs fill the air,
Each one more grand than a bear.

I chase them on my bike,
Hoping for a fun hike.
But they swarm like wild bees,
It's just a laugh, if you please!

Daffodils' Serenade at Dawn

Under the bright sun's yawn,
Wobbling blooms greet the dawn.
They giggle in the breeze,
Spread laughs among the trees.

A whiff of springtime charm,
They wave to me, no harm.
But watch your step, oh friend,
Or you may just start to blend!

Sneezes crowd the morning air,
As I dance without a care.
Yellow hats all a-sway,
It's a pollen cabaret!

The daffs and I all play,
We giggle the day away.
With every little whiff,
I feel like a flower tiff!

Secrets Carried on the Wind

Whispers from the trees fly,
With secrets from the sky.
Little bits of chatter talk,
While I take a cheerful walk.

They loop and spin, what a joke,
Like a soaring, giddy cloak.
I wave my arms in delight,
They peek and dash out of sight.

"Why must you tickle me so?"
I ask the breeze, "Take it slow!"
Yet, with a giggle I find,
Mischief blooms—oh, so kind!

The earth and sky collide,
Where funny secrets bide.
With each puff, I'm in a whirl,
It's just nature's quirky twirl!

The Artistry of Nature's Gift

A sneeze, a sniff, some flair,
The tiny dancers float with care.
In every breeze, a tickly tease,
Making us laugh and sneeze with ease.

The flowers laugh, they rock and sway,
As tiny bits join in the play.
With every puff, they bring delight,
And make us dance in sheer delight.

The bees partake in this grand ball,
With honeyed tunes that charm us all.
But oh, beware the sunny days,
When nature plays its funny ways!

So raise a glass to playful spring,
To all the joys that it can bring.
In every laugh and every cheer,
We find the joy of this time of year.

Colors That Kiss the Sky

Oh look, the colors fly around,
With little floats that stir the ground.
They twirl and spin, such lively sights,
Causing giggles on bright days and nights.

A gust of wind, a swirling dance,
A cheeky move, now watch it prance.
They play hide and seek on trees,
Giving all noses a tickly sneeze.

Sunshine smiles, and all is bright,
While nature teases left and right.
Each hue awakes the jolly sound,
Creating laughter all around.

With paints so vivid, skyscapes tease,
Sprinkling joy like dandelion breeze.
In colors wild, they seem to play,
In nature's game, we laugh all day.

Tender Caress of Springtime's Breath

Breezy whispers through the field,
Tiny bits now gently yield.
Each step we take, they hitch a ride,
With chuckles shared, we feel alive.

The trees are giggling, can't you see?
With every gust, they dance with glee.
A tickle here, a laugh out loud,
As nature's jesters weave a shroud.

The sun beams down, a playful wink,
While flowers bloom and icy drinks.
They play tag with the careless air,
While we all stop and laugh and stare.

So here's to spring, so full of jest,
With every whirl, we feel so blessed.
Laughter carried on the breeze,
Nature's gift, our hearts it frees.

Fluttering Whims of Nature's Heart

In the garden, flutter and flit,
A lively chaos, not a bit quit.
With tiny whirlwinds darting near,
They tease our noses, bring forth cheer.

The daisies chuckle in vibrant hues,
While sunshine bathes in bright, warm views.
A dandelion's mischievous grin,
As sprightly gusts sweep nonsense in.

Each twist and turn, a playful chase,
Where laughter sprinkles this magical space.
With whispers soft, the breezes call,
Join the dance, embrace it all!

So let us laugh with nature's flair,
In every breeze, joy fills the air.
With winks and wiggles, we take part,
In fluttering whims of nature's heart.

The Softest Raiment of Nature

In gardens lush, a sneak attack,
Tiny dancers start to stack.
Wings aflutter, come and play,
The softest raiment on display.

Tickled noses, sneezing spree,
A family joins, just wait and see!
With laughter loud, they run about,
In nature's attire, they twist and shout.

Breezes giggle, tease the trees,
Coughing, wheezing, 'Oh geez, oh geez!'
A sneaky game, it's pure delight,
With hats of yellow, a silly sight!

So here we dance, in sun-kissed cheer,
The world's a stage, the show is clear.
With every laugh, and every trace,
A joyful romp in this lively place.

Threads of Life in Silent Currents

In whispered winds, where secrets blend,
Ghostly threads begin to wend.
With every breeze, a tickle found,
It dances lightly on the ground.

Kittens chase the fluttering spots,
While adults cough and tie their knots.
"Oh dear!" they shout, in playful jest,
With tissues poised, there's no time to rest!

A sneeze erupts, a wild surprise,
Creating magic, in all our eyes.
As laughter spills, we sway and spin,
The threads of life, where fun begins.

So let us revel, and not despair,
In this wild ride through fragrant air.
We'll laugh and sing, 'til shadows loom,
In this tapestry of joyous bloom.

The Hidden Magic of the Tides

With every wave, a twist, a foible,
The seashells giggle, oh what a noble!
They shimmer and shine, a wobbly sight,
A beach ballet, oh what delight!

Sudden sneezes as grains take flight,
Allergies dance, oh what a fright!
But laughter rings across the shore,
As waves crash on, we ask for more.

A rogue seagull steals a sandwich slice,
And dodges sneezes, oh how nice!
In salty air, we spin and sway,
Chasing the giggles of another day.

So grab a friend, let the tide decide,
With each new gust, let laughter glide.
In hidden magic, we'll find our way,
In a whimsical world where we love to play.

Blossoms in a Whispering World

In whispers sweet, the flowers speak,
With colors bright, they play hide and seek.
A cheeky breeze, a giggling tease,
Inviting all, to join with ease.

Beware the sneeze, oh watch your nose!
For laughter blooms wherever it goes.
A petal party with all our friends,
This noisy romp that never ends!

From daisies bright to tulips tall,
Their colors flash like nature's call.
Once dignified, now a clumsy blur,
As pollen pranks begin to stir!

So let us dance in this laughing field,
A whimsical world, the heart's great shield.
In every breath, a story shared,
In blossoms bright, hilariously cared.

Treetops' Dusty Reverie

Up high where the breezes play,
Tiny specks begin to sway.
Birds with sneezes, oh what fun,
Coughing gifts from the golden sun.

Trees wear coats of yellow hue,
Wiggling in the warm sun's view.
Squirrels dance with sneaky flair,
Chasing fluff that fills the air.

In the park, a sneeze erupts,
A startled dog, then one abrupt.
Everyone's a-nose surveying,
As blossoms play their subtle saying.

Children giggle, running wild,
At swirls of scents, they feel beguiled.
A world of laughter, that's the theme,
With cheeky tracks from nature's dream.

Starlit Wishes on the Wind

Underneath the moon's bright gleam,
Fluffy wonders make us beam.
Dancing through our nighttime chat,
Wishes floating like a cat.

Fireflies blink in playful jest,
While cheeky breezes pass the test.
Hearts aflutter, snorkel-style,
Chasing dreams for just a while.

Jumping twirls and silly spins,
As nature's magic softly wins.
With every laugh, we breathe the light,
Through sparkly giggles, our delight.

Winks from night and whispers cheer,
As starry wishes draw us near.
Adventure swirls with a giggle sound,
In the laughter-rich, tree-filled ground.

Celestial Whispers of the Wild

In the woods a ruckus grows,
As fluffs depart from leafy prose.
Creatures clad in fine disguise,
Tickled by the breeze that flies.

Bunnies hop with sneaky flair,
Chasing clouds that twirl and care.
Frogs in tuxedos croak a song,
As nature's giggles carry strong.

Breezes tease the grass so bold,
Telling tales that can't be told.
While wise old owls find their perch,
Swapping stories in their lurch.

Laughter echoes through the trees,
In a world of playful ease.
As gentle whispers tumble loud,
Nature's joy, forever proud.

Gentle Sighs in Nature's Breath

With every step, a ticklish tease,
From mystery clouds that dance with ease.
Leaves chuckle under sunlit grace,
As laughter spins in nature's face.

Silly bees, they buzz around,
In floral games where joy is found.
A dandelion took a spin,
With gusty laughs, the fun begins.

Windy whispers, cheeky grins,
As nature's party, loud it spins.
Frolicsome friends in leafy skirts,
Join the frolic where laughter flirts.

In this realm, let giggles flow,
Where earth's own warmth can surely grow.
While time takes flight and fun ensues,
Join the whimsy, we cannot lose.

Whirls of Nature's Promise

Tiny dancers drift about,
On a mission, no doubt.
They tickle noses, what a game!
Sneezes follow, ain't that the same?

Laughter bubbles in the breeze,
As allergies hold us at ease.
The sun shines bright, all is well,
While we wave to the sneezy spell.

Little fluffballs, oh so sly,
Whirling 'round with a cheeky eye.
Promising blooms, a funny plight,
Yet leaves us sniffling through the night.

With wiggles in the meadow's dance,
They flirt with flowers, add some chance.
Nature's jesters on the fly,
Tickling noses as they pass by.

A Dance of Sunshine Whispers

Sunshine giggles, a jolly tune,
As gentle breezes play at noon.
Whimsical sprouts begin to tease,
While we fumble, trying to sneeze.

The golden rays weave through the trees,
Chasing shadows, dodging bees.
Fluffy sprites flit here and there,
Mixing mischief with fresh air.

A twirl of giggles fills the sky,
As little bits of joy drift by.
Frolicking grass, a merry sight,
As nature's tricks spark pure delight.

Come join the fun, oh what a treat!
Dancing spores that skip and greet.
With every step, a sneeze or two,
Nature whispers, how do you do?

The Breath of Verdant Awakening

The greens unfold, a funny sight,
As morning sneezes greet the light.
Sprouts of mischief laugh and play,
They scatter giggles along the way.

With every cough, a chuckle stirs,
As nature tickles, oh how it blurs!
A dash of green, a spark of cream,
In this whacky, wild, sneezing dream.

The trees exchange their silly notes,
While we try to sail our boats.
Each floating whim, a burst of cheer,
As we all wheeze and hold our dear.

Characters clad in chlorophyll,
Play hide and seek, a laughter thrill.
With silly games of smell and sound,
The verdant chorus spins around.

Seeds Carried by Hope's Wind

The wind is giggling, full of cheer,
As tiny travelers roam near.
Seeds on a sailboat, a fluffy crew,
They ride the breeze, just passing through.

Whirls of joy in the summer glow,
They party hearty, putting on a show.
With winks and nudges, they wave goodbye,
While unsuspecting eyes let out a sigh.

From dandelions, a sneezy plight,
To swirling whispers of sheer delight.
Each poof and puff, a playful tease,
Messing with noses like it's a breeze.

Sprinkling laughter in every bite,
As nature's jesters shine so bright.
So here's the truth, with a gentle grin,
Life's more fun with a sneezy spin!

Nature's Colorful Confetti

Tiny tickles on my nose,
A sneeze erupts and chaos grows.
Sunshine flirts with dancing light,
As sneezes echo, what a sight!

Buzzy bugs in party hats,
Flit and flutter, where they're at?
They join the fun with all their flair,
While I chase them in despair.

Colors swirl, a vibrant mess,
Nature's prank, I must confess.
Sneezing children run about,
In this game, there's no doubt!

As I dodge the whimsical spray,
I laugh and sigh, come what may.
A fragrant cloud that brings delight,
Who knew grass could cause this plight?

Luminescent Threads of Growth

A golden trail across the lane,
It tickles toes, but brings up pain.
With every step, I'm on the brink,
Of charming blooms that make me think!

Swaying petals of the bold,
Making sporting events so uncontrolled.
When the breeze shakes their parade,
Even the bees seem quite dismayed.

A brilliant mess, I must report,
With blooms that love to cavort and sport!
Nature's hide and seek game's on,
Each little sneeze lights up the dawn.

Yet I tread lightly, do my best,
What's that tickle? I jest, I jest!
With bright confetti in my hair,
Oh what fun, this enchantment rare!

Swaying Spheres of Enchantment

Bouncing balls of yellow cheer,
They float like dreams, oh dear, oh dear!
I chase these orbs across the park,
With every leap, I miss the mark.

In laughter, I spin around,
As nature's giggle does abound.
The wind it teases, what a joy,
But here comes chaos – oh boy, oh boy!

Dizzy from the chase I take,
Suddenly, I'm a human quake!
Swinging round with wild delight,
"Catch me if you can!" I indict.

These merry spheres keep leading me,
To sneezes that are quite the spree.
With snot-filled smiles, I proclaim,
In this wild game, there's no shame!

Nature's Celestial Confetti

A sprinkle here, a sprinkle there,
This mischievous dust fills the air.
With each small gust, I dance and sway,
A cosmic party gone astray!

Little stars from daisies leap,
Into my drink - oh what a creep!
I sip, I choke, and then I laugh,
This wild brew is nature's half!

Around me whirl a yellow show,
As I ponder, "Where'd it go?"
These creatures laugh, with twinkling eyes,
I trip on joy - what a surprise!

In this festival of laughter bright,
I find my way in the sunlight.
With tiny bursts floating wide,
Nature's playfulness can't be denied!

A Conspiracy of Flora's Flight

In the meadow, flowers scheme,
With plans to cast a fuzzy dream.
The bees conspire, wearing shades,
In a buzzing dance, their wits displayed.

Lilies laugh, as daisies wink,
They share secrets over a drink.
A dandelion whispers bold,
'We're the party, watch it unfold!'

The breeze joins in with a cheeky grin,
Swirling and twirling, it's a win.
Petals take flight, like confetti spread,
While garden gnomes nod their heads.

Just watch your nose with these tiny foes,
They're plotting chaos, goodness knows!
With every sneeze, they all will cheer,
"Another laugh, we've spread good cheer!"

Secrets Strewn Across the Sky

A fluffy cloud in the bright blue,
Says, 'Here comes mischief, howdy-do!'
With tiny whispers, secrets fly,
As colors dance and laughter sighs.

The tulips gossip, with petals wide,
While tulip tops take a colorful ride.
The cosmos giggle, oh what a sight,
As whispering breezes play all night.

The yellow swirls when the sun breaks free,
As bees do the cha-cha with wild glee.
Every gust is a jester's call,
With nature's laughter, it touches all.

So grab your hat, don't lose your shoe,
The sky is in on the prank, it's true!
In a zany dance that's hard to ignore,
Join the sky's party, say 'more, more, more!'

Voyage of the Dandelion Seeds

On a journey swift, the seeds embark,
In tiny boats, they sail and spark.
A breeze that giggles, tickles their side,
As they leave the ground, finding their glide.

'Anchors away!' one seed does declare,
While others scatter without a care.
A map made of wishes, their travel guide,
For the wild adventures they boost with pride.

Through sunlight and shadow, they zoom and twirl,
They hop over fences, give flowers a whirl.
With glorious laughter, they dance in the air,
Each tumble a treasure, beyond compare.

They land in gardens, to everyone's surprise,
Planting their dreams where laughter flies.
"Oh look, a comedian, watch him float!"
A jaunty farewell, their jests in full quote!

Harmony of Windswept Colors

A rainbow mishap, oh what a sight,
Colors collide, giggles take flight.
The violets tease the roses so bold,
While chamomile smiles, soft and gold.

The winds sweep in, a playful tease,
Twirling hues with delicate ease.
The sun's a joker, casting rays,
Painting the garden in whimsical ways.

Tulips don't mind, they're all for fun,
Spinning tall tales under the sun.
A chorus of colors in joyous glee,
Where every misstep brings mirth to be.

So don your cap, and join the spree,
As petal parties brew wild and free.
In this merry dance, we share our cheer,
In the harmony where colors appear!

Nature's Glittering Farewell

A hint of gold, it drifts and flies,
Making noses twitch, oh what a surprise!
Bees wear it proudly, like a little crown,
While sneezes echo all over town.

In sunny meadows, it dances with glee,
A tickle in the air, and this is the key.
Every spring event needs a lively guest,
With laughter and snorts, we surely are blessed.

The trees throw a party with a sneezy cheer,
Under bright skies, we laugh and we leer.
As we dodge the cloud, like a comedy act,
Who knew nature's jest could be so exact?

So here's to the fun, the giggles and wheeze,
This sparkly stuff blowing with ease.
Let's shake off our worries, let's dance on a dare,
For life's little joys are sprinkled everywhere!

A Journey Through Sweet Breaths

A drift of fluff, oh what's that I feel?
Is it a dancer, or just a big deal?
Floating so freely, like confetti in time,
I laugh at the tickle, oh isn't it prime?

The breeze plays a tune, oh, a whimsical song,
With each little wave, we all sing along.
The trees giggle softly, the grasses take sway,
In this sunny ballet, we lose track of day.

Like tiny fairies with wings of delight,
It brightens our path, oh, what a sight!
With every sweet breath, a tinge of zest,
Making spring's antics an absolute fest.

So come take a trip, on this fluffy delight,
Where laughter erupts in the warm golden light.
A journey of whimsy, in nature's own style,
Sprinkling joy freely, making us smile!

The Magic in the Air's Embrace

Oh, what's this magic that tickles my nose?
It swirls like a dancer in wonderful clothes.
With each little breeze, it throws me a prank,
And here comes a sneeze—oh dear, how I drank!

In gardens of laughter, the fun just ignites,
With each joyful giggle, we dance and take flights.
The world's painted gold, like a joke we all share,
As we wave to the fluff in the warm summer air.

Little whispers of joy float past in the light,
Turning frowns to chuckles, oh, what a delight!
The whimsical jesters make nature's parade,
A comedic adventure we'd never trade.

So when you're out walking, take note of the fun,
In the embrace of bright magic, we're never done.
Let laughter explode, let the good times roll,
For this is the air that tickles the soul!

Lush Horizons Painted Bright

In fields of fun where the wild things play,
Sparkles fall softly, what a crazy display!
The colors of laughter, the scent of delight,
All creatures unite in this whimsical flight.

With every small shuffle, the ground gives a cheer,
From blushing blooms bursting, oh, what do we hear?
A melody of joy, as the sun shines so bright,
Oh, let's capture the magic, hold on tight!

Each step is a chuckle, each breath a delight,
With some silly tussles, we dance in the light.
It's a garden of giggles, a riotous show,
Where the world wears a grin, come join in the glow!

So here's to lush views, to the bright and absurd,
To the colorful antics of this feathered bird.
Let's giggle and chatter, as we bask in the light,
For in this hilarity, horizons feel right!

Nectar's Gentle Breeze

Little bees do jig and jive,
Tickling noses, they arrive.
With a buzz that's quite a tease,
Drifting softly on the breeze.

Sneezing humans, watch your step,
Laughter echoes, what a prep!
Nature's joke, a fluffy spree,
Allergies become the key.

Yellow clouds swirl in delight,
Dancing under morning light.
With each gust, a gleeful hoot,
Nature's prank, oh what a scoot!

So when you sniffle, just remember,
It's a party, not a bender.
Join the fun, don't hide away,
Embrace the tickles—come what may!

In the Dance of Sweet Dust

Tiny twirls in the spring sun,
Check the outfits, everyone.
Fluffy clouds in pastel hues,
Watch out folks, it's a wild snooze!

Sneezes come in rhythmic beats,
While the flowers tap their feets.
A laughter trail, what a sight,
Pollen party, pure delight!

Breezy whispers, giggles float,
As bees don their tiny coat.
Jumping high in joyful glee,
Nature's jesters, oh so free!

The world's a stage, and we're the crew,
Watch as colors change their view.
Butterflies join, oh what a laugh,
Nature's silly, vibrant path!

Laughter of Flowers Unfurled

Blossoms giggle in the field,
Their cheeky charm is revealed.
As the wind blows in a swirl,
Petals dance and softly twirl.

Bumblebees wear hats of gold,
Sharing secrets, sweet and bold.
Nature's jest, a cheery spell,
Belly laughs from every bell!

With a tickle on the nose,
Comes a smile, sweet as a rose.
Colors clash in bright display,
What a raucous, joyful day!

So join the blooms, don't just stare,
Join the fun, don't sit and spare.
In this moment, wild and free,
Laughter lives in harmony!

The Golden Kiss of Blossoms

Golden kisses from above,
Like sweet whispers of true love.
Chasing giggles through the air,
A ballet on a spring affair.

Buzzy pals in frenzied flight,
Turn every frown into delight.
Sneezing fits are all the rage,
Nature's comedy on stage!

Through gardens where the colors bloom,
Comes a tickle from the gloom.
With each gust, a happy cheer,
Join the dance—no need to fear!

So let the laughter fill your heart,
With nature's joy, we play our part.
In every bloom and playful risk,
The golden dance, oh what a whisk!

Dance of the Sunlit Spirits

In the garden where giggles bloom,
Tiny dancers twirl in the room.
They wear hats of yellow and gold,
Whispering secrets, ages old.

With every jiggle and jive,
They make the flowers feel alive.
Bouncing around like balls of fluff,
Nature's party can't get enough!

A waltz with bees in happy fight,
Sipping nectar, oh what a sight!
They wear their masks, all fuzzy and bright,
Under the sun, it feels so right.

As the breeze carries tales of cheer,
The flowers laugh, they've got no fear.
In the hustle of this lively sphere,
The sunlit spirits always appear!

Threads of Life on a Whisper

Threads of joy float through the blue,
Tickling noses, just like a shoe.
With a giggle, they waltz by,
Leaving us wondering, oh why?

The daisies chuckle, the roses grin,
As fuzzy beings start to spin.
Each little thread, a playful tease,
Rustling softly through the leaves.

Bees in tutus, on tiny feet,
Join in the chaos, can't be beat!
Nature's threads hold laughter tight,
In this dance of pure delight.

Invisible strings pull us near,
For a moment, we toss out our fear.
With a wink, and a hopeful cheer,
Life's gentle charms are here, oh dear!

Echoes of Flora's Heartbeat

Listen closely to the beat,
Where leafy laughter finds its seat.
Giggles echo through the glade,
In this playful, leafy parade.

Sunshine bounces, tickling leaves,
As nature dances, she believes.
Every flower sways with flair,
In sync with whispers in the air.

Bumblebees in disco boots,
Spin their way through blooming shoots.
Petal confetti flies so high,
Raining down from the laughter sky.

While the world spins, we hold tight,
To echoes of joy, shared in flight.
In the pulse of green, we delight,
As Flora's heart keeps beating bright!

Soft Touch of Nature's Brush

Nature paints with a playful hand,
Tickling vines across the land.
With every stroke, she starts to laugh,
Creating a colorful photograph.

Soft whispers pass through the trees,
A gentle tickle in the breeze.
With every rustle, joy takes flight,
Creating colors, pure delight.

Tiny feet add their own flair,
As butterflies dance without a care.
Nature's canvas smiles in sun,
With every brush stroke, we have fun!

In this gallery, laughter flows,
With every petal, joy grows.
They say, "Come join us, don't be shy!"
With the soft touch, we reach for the sky!

Textures of Gentle Awakening

Tiny dancers float through the breeze,
Tickling noses, bringing you to your knees.
A sneeze here, a laugh there, oh what a scene,
Nature's confetti—who knew it could be so keen?

Colors burst forth in a grand parade,
Chasing each other, they twirl and fade.
You think they play fair? Oh, that's quite a joke,
They dodge and they dive like a playful bloke!

Butterflies giggle in shades so bright,
As bees hum their tunes, oh what a delight.
They buzz and they bounce, share in the fun,
It's a carnival game where no one's outrun!

With every soft flutter, a chuckle rings true,
A tickle of laughter from me unto you.
In the morning's embrace, we all dance along,
As the world dusts itself off, singing spring's song.

Gifts Wrapped in Soft Petals

A package of joy falls from the sky,
With glittery bits that make you sigh.
Wrapped up in colors, a gift to behold,
Open it gently—watch those jokes unfold!

The bees are like bouncers at this lush event,
Guarding the treasures they feel are well spent.
They laugh as they dance, spinning round with glee,
While you sneeze and you wheeze—oh, what a spree!

Silly soft whispers blow through the trees,
As starlings consult on how best to tease.
A chuckle erupts when a petal lands smack,
Right on your cheek—oh, don't take it back!

So grab your hat tight, and join in the jest,
As nature's prankster puts humor to test.
With petals as pillows, we'll cozy up here,
And laugh till the sun sets, till night's drawing near.

The Echo of Sweetness Above

There's a sugar rush lurking in each gentle breeze,
With whispers of cupcakes and honey-filled trees.
The air is a feast, can you smell the delight?
But hold your nose tight—oh what a sight!

A raindrop of laughter takes flight without care,
As daisies suggest a wild, silly hair.
Who knew a flower could giggle so loud?
Each bloom a comedian, drawing a crowd!

Strawberries swing from their vines in a chorus,
Promising sweetness, like a fruit-loving florist.
Watch them shake hands with the cheeky dandelions,
Swap silly secrets from quirky French lions!

The echoes of sweetness won't fade anytime,
As sugarplum visions dance soft like a rhyme.
Join this odd party beneath cobalt skies,
Where laughter's the currency, and joy never dies.

Whispers of Spring's Embrace

A tickle of breezes plays hide and seek,
As flowers gossip, each bloom's got a peek.
They chat and they chuckle, oh what a rumor,
That spring's just a jester with grandiose humor!

Every fluttering leaf joins the fun,
While soaking in warmth from the smile of the sun.
The grass makes a squabble, it tickles your toes,
Inviting you in for sweet, silly shows!

The clouds play tag with a wink and a grin,
As rain drops hint at a playful chagrin.
Dance through the garden, with snickers so wild,
Like a mischievous kid, nature's own child!

So here's to the giggles that springtime will share,
In the grand theater, a comedic affair.
With whispers of joy, let's clap and rejoice,
For laughter's the magic—let's all raise our voice!

Breezy Hues of Renewal

With dancing seeds that fly and twirl,
The sneezing starts with every whirl.
A patch of green with colors bright,
As noses twitch in pure delight.

The bees are buzzing, oh what luck,
While allergies say, "What the pluck!"
The flowers wink and grin so wide,
As we sneeze and run, nowhere to hide.

Light Kisses from the Garden

Tiny bits on silky wings,
Nature's jest, the laughter brings.
A breeze, a giggle in the breeze,
While we swat away with frantic pleas.

With every sniffle, there's a cheer,
For splashes of yellow draw us near.
The garden's prank, a gentle tease,
As we dance around and try to sneeze.

Invincible Dust of Life

Invisible foes from flower beds,
Crafting chaos in our heads.
We leap and dodge, a comic show,
As errant blasts make laughter flow.

Tiny bits, a game so grand,
As we swipe with a desperate hand.
Nature's confetti, wild and free,
Tickling noses like a jubilee.

Cadence of the Forgotten Gardens

In secret nooks where blooms abound,
A tickle here, a sneeze profound.
Amidst the weeds, we dance and sway,
In a hilarious springtime ballet.

With eyes that water like a stream,
We laugh and choke, it's quite the scene.
That lovely dust, our constant friends,
A comic tale that never ends.

Embrace of Gilded Flurries

The bees are buzzing, oh what a scene,
With tiny backpacks, they're quite the machine.
They dance with glee on the springtime breeze,
In petals of laughter, they flutter with ease.

A sneeze turns into a laugh at my plight,
Everywhere I look, it's a colorful sight.
My nose does a jig, it's a tickling spree,
Who knew that a flower could humor me?

With sunshine pouring, the world's a delight,
The little specks glimmer, a magical flight.
Life's in full bloom, can't help but to share,
A giggle erupts from the joys in the air.

As nature's confetti falls all around,
I laugh when I see the chaos abound.
I tiptoe through blossoms with quite the flair,
In a world of giggles, who wouldn't dare?

Secrets in the Airwaves

What whispers they carry, those buzzards so sly,
Like tiny spies, they flit and they fly.
They tease and they taunt, with their sweet little tricks,
Collecting the secrets, like mischievous kicks.

A hop and a skip, they buzz past my head,
I chase them around on my picnic spread.
With humor they sprinkle, those little things dance,
As I'm swatting wildly, without a chance.

The flutter and flicker, such playful delight,
Brings joy to my heart on this sunshiny night.
In a meadow of giggles, I roll and I sway,
These tiny pranksters, leading me astray.

With a tickle and grin, they swirl all about,
In a whirl of existence, they twist and they shout.
My allergies flare, but I can't seem to care,
For the laughter they bring is divinely rare.

The Language of Budding Flora

In the garden of chatter, the blooms softly speak,
With whispers of humor, they play hide and seek.
The daisies are giggling, the roses do sway,
It's a floral fiesta in a humorous way.

I sneeze at the petals, they shrug and they sigh,
"Come join in the fun!" they seem to reply.
The tulips wink bright with a cheeky allure,
While the pansies grumble, "Oh, can't we be pure?"

From daffodil jokes to jokes about thyme,
The flora in unison creates quite a rhyme.
With every small breeze, they tickle my nose,
It's a garden of laughter, where anything goes.

As the sun starts to set and the shadows grow tall,
I witness a circus, nature's grand ball.
In this whimsical turf, where flowers would dare,
I burst out in laughter, breathe in the air!

Ethereal Drifts of Life

A swirl of bright colors, a joyous parade,
The world is a canvas, nature's charade.
With each little flurry, I'm caught in the fun,
As the gold-dusted breezes begin their sweet run.

My nose is a bridge to the giggles they send,
Through the air they float, all sprightly and bend.
Like tiny comedians, they brighten the day,
In a dance of delight, they twirl and they play.

I follow their trail, like a friend on the run,
As they dart through the daisies, it's all just so fun.
A nose full of mischief and laughter so bright,
In the whimsical air, everything feels right.

As twilight approaches with stars up above,
I ponder the joy, the laughter, the love.
These delicate drifters, they float and they care,
With a spark in my heart, I embrace what they share.

Tides of Floral Offering

With whispers from the blossom blooms,
A sneeze erupts, oh how it looms.
The bees all laugh, they start to dance,
While humans cough and wheeze by chance.

A gust of breeze, a floral jest,
It tickles noses, no time to rest.
Double sneeze? It's quite the show,
Cheers to the flowers, down below!

The sun is shining, laugh we might,
As nature's pranksters take their flight.
We dance and sneeze, a comic plight,
Oh, the joys of springtime's light!

With tissues ready, we charge ahead,
Oh sprightly blooms, you've sprung your thread.
In gardens bright, the fun begins,
Who knew that flowers made such sins?

Aether's Tiny Gifts

Dusky clouds of fragrant cheer,
Tickling noses, oh dear, oh dear!
Like little gremlins on a spree,
They take their aim, just wait and see!

The daffodils, with golden threads,
Whisper secrets as they spread.
A surprise attack on hapless souls,
Their giggles echo, in joyful trolls.

In summer's warmth, they find their glee,
They float around, a wild jubilee.
With every giggle, chuckle, and laugh,
They're on a mission, oh what a craft!

And if you sneeze, just join the fun,
A party starts, when all is done.
They know your name, they're here to play,
Aether's tiny gifts, come what may!

Nectar's Silent Messengers

Little spies in the bright blue sky,
On the breeze, they rise and fly.
Trickster buds, with yellow crowns,
Watch out below, they'll bring you frowns!

A giggle, a gasp, here comes the swarm,
With cute intentions, not a hint of harm.
They sprinkle mischief by the hour,
In fields of gold, they find their power.

Sneezes erupt like carnival tunes,
A sudden shock, beneath the moons.
With laughter echoing in the air,
Who knew these gifts would lead to despair?

So here's to all those sneaky thugs,
The silent messengers, full of hugs.
In every tickle, a cheer we take,
Thank you, blossoms, for all your shake!

The Scent of Blossoms Unfurled

Oh the scent, it wafts and swirls,
Tickling noses, the laughter twirls.
Who knew blooms were such jokers?
Causing chaos for all the smokers!

As petals shake in the sun's sweet kiss,
We inhale deep, but it's a hit or miss.
With each mighty sneeze, we can't control,
The hilarity takes over, a rising toll.

From daisies to roses, a fragrant strife,
They dance around with glimmers of life.
Chasing us with whimsical tease,
Who knew flowers could bring us unease?

Yet through the giggles, we find delight,
As blossoms bloom in the warming light.
So raise a glass to the floral jest,
For in their chaos, we find the best!

Golden Haze of Awakening

In the morn, a sneeze erupts,
As tiny specks begin their dance,
My nose now itches, what's this?
Springtime's prank, a wild romance.

Butterflies laugh, on flowers they play,
While I chase the whispers of sunny delight,
Each step I take's a comedic ballet,
In this yellow fog, I lose my sight.

Rolling in grass, I trip on a bee,
With my allergies flaring, oh what a sight!
The flowers chuckle, they're teasing me,
In this golden haze, nothing feels right!

Yet through the sneezes and sniffs I find,
A joy in this madness, a splash of delight,
For though it may tickle and drive me blind,
This golden haze makes everything bright!

The Fluttering Gold

The air's alive, with a golden glow,
It dances 'round like a clown on a spree,
My allergies joke, as they steal the show,
With each wheeze and cough, they're laughing at me.

A ladybug struts, in sheer confidence found,
While I stumble forward, a fit of the wild,
This buzzing chaos, it knows no bound,
As I swat at the air, a clumsy child.

Sneezing and giggling, I trip on my toes,
That golden confetti, it's quite the affair,
Every tickle that comes, why, everybody knows,
Springtime's a jester with tricks to declare!

Yet here I remain, with my goofy grace,
Embracing the chaos, my nature's own song,
For amidst all the joy, there's a smile on my face,
In this fluttering gold, it's where I belong!

Essence of Blooming Dreams

With the dawn, dreams begin to sprout,
Like confetti thrown in the festival flair,
In a sneeze-filled dance, I prance about,
Chasing the magic, but barely aware.

A bumblebee buzzes, wearing a crown,
While I jump and dodge, a quirky routine,
As flowers giggle with petals of brown,
The essence of spring is a sight to be seen.

Dive into foliage, I tumble and roll,
Comforted by scents that tickle my nose,
Laughter erupts as I lose control,
In this whimsical world, where anything goes!

Yet even through chaos, my heart lifts in cheer,
For in taking the plunge, I find such delight,
With the essence around, it's all crystal clear,
These blooming dreams make the world feel just right!

Soft Kernels in the Breeze

In the breeze, little kernels flit,
A thousand giggles from nature's own play,
As I chase them down, I just can't quite sit,
These soft little devils, they ruin my day!

With each little sneeze, I'm flung into air,
Dancing and spinning, a comedic delight,
The grains of spring whisper without a care,
And laughter erupts, a true slapstick fight!

Hopping like rabbits, I join the parade,
While butterflies swirl, they've come for the show,
My antics confirmed, in this plush charade,
"Join in!" they seem to say, "Just let go!"

At last, I relent, surrender to fun,
Caught in a swirl of nature's wise tease,
For these soft little kernels bring joy by the ton,
And with a grand chuckle, I dance in the breeze!

A Tapestry of Fragrant Flecks

Tiny specks are flying by,
Gathering on your cheek so sly.
You wave your hands, they start a dance,
A sneaky whim, no second chance.

Oh look! A sneeze, a sudden blast,
The flowers laugh, they're having a blast.
A cloud of giggles fills the air,
As all the colors swirl with flair.

Mismatched socks in brilliant hues,
Tickled noses and wiggly shoes.
The bees are buzzing, quite a show,
While we all jump, dodging the flow.

In this game of hide and seek,
The bits of cheer make us all cheek.
What's that? A tickle in the nose,
A laugh erupts, who knows where it goes!

Beneath the Canopy of Color

Underneath the rainbow bright,
The tickly bits take off in flight.
Dancing 'round like cheeky sprites,
Whirling up in joyful heights.

A friend thinks he can catch a few,
But winds of wits just whisk him through.
With every tiptoe, leaps, and bounds,
The painted flecks just swirl around.

Laughter echoes, oh what fun,
Chasing flecks, they start to run.
Each color lands, a playful tease,
As giggles ride the playful breeze.

A sneeze erupts—a startling spree,
"Excuse me!" shouts my friend with glee.
The flowers chuckle in their beds,
As we retreat and scratch our heads!

Scented Dreams Drifting by

In the garden, dreams ignite,
Whispers flutter, day turns bright.
Fragrant trails weave here and there,
Sprinkling giggles into the air.

A butterfly with quite a flair,
Tries to catch the flecks up there.
It twirls and spins, a comical sight,
In this chase, we lose the fight.

With noses twitching, up we leap,
Trying hard, but giggles seep.
Each little sneeze, a joyful sound,
As dancing flecks come twirling 'round.

They swirl like confetti, oh so spry,
The world turns colorful, oh my, oh my!
With every hiccup and every cheer,
The joyful bits bring laughter near.

Trails of Gold on a Gentle Zephyr

On the breeze, a golden trail,
A band of yellow, oh so frail.
We chase them down, but they just flee,
A wiggly race, oh what a spree.

With every step, they pirouette,
Tickled noses, can't forget!
Caught off guard, we start to sneeze,
The flowers grin as we feel the tease.

A gentle tug of laughter spins,
All in fun, as joy begins.
We form a team, the hunt is on,
Those playful flecks, they dance till dawn.

As evening falls, we laugh and sway,
Chasing dreams at close of day.
With every giggle, cheers resound,
In this wild world, joy is found!

Secrets of the Budding World

Tiny grains on a breeze,
Fluttering with giggly ease.
Chatting flowers, a buzzing crew,
Whispering secrets to me and you.

Petals tickle the silly bees,
Doing cartwheels with utmost glee.
Nature's confetti, a joyful parade,
Who knew springtime could be such a charade?

Buzz and wiggle, don't be shy,
Watch the dandelions happily fly.
With each sneeze, a story's told,
Of nature's antics, bright and bold.

So let's laugh with the garden's cheer,
As we dance to the tunes we hear.
In this world where laughter blends,
The secrets of life are laughed at, my friends.

Touch of the Gentle Harvest

When the sun gives a wink and a grin,
Drifty fun begins once again.
Golden dust on a lazy breeze,
Twirling like dancers among the trees.

The bumblebees with their silly dance,
Wobble around as if in a trance.
They sip and giggle, wiggling their rear,
"Oh dear!" they shout, "Can you believe we're here?"

Carrying parcels of joy galore,
They stop for a chat, then off they soar.
Frolicsome flights, a harvest that's sweet,
With every bloom, a delightful treat.

So grab a friend and join the chase,
To celebrate nature's playful grace.
In laughter, we'll bask, as we glean, oh so bright,
The touch of the gentle harvest takes flight!

Journeys Beyond Blossom and Bough

Adventure calls on a sunny day,
With giggles tangling in the fray.
Floofy fluff floats without a care,
Decorating all in happy flair.

Critters hop and skip with zest,
In the great outdoors, they feel blessed.
Each little waft carries a joke,
Mother Nature packs laughs in every stroke.

Buds and blooms gossip away,
Swapping tales of breezy play.
"Don't be shy!" the petals sing,
"Join us now, let your heart take wing!"

Across the fields, they travel wide,
With hearty chuckles, they drift and slide.
Life's a circus of giggles and fun,
In journeys bright, we all become one!

The Sweetness of Golden Swirls

In the garden, sweet whirls abound,
Buzzing creatures spin round and round.
A sprinkle of laughter, a dash of cheer,
Golden swirls waft, oh so near.

A sneaky breeze tickles the grass,
While flowers shout, "Come join our class!"
They gather round for a pollen party,
Where every laugh is downright hearty.

With a twist and a twirl in the sun,
Nature's jesters invite everyone.
Ticklish petals toss jokes in the air,
As giggles dance everywhere, oh rare!

So let's celebrate this merry swirl,
In a world where chuckles and joy unfurl.
With each silly breeze that flits and twirls,
We find sweet laughter in golden swirls.

www.ingramcontent.com/pod-product-compliance
Lightning Source LLC
Chambersburg PA
CBHW050317100526
44585CB00016BA/1560